TRUST MORE
FEAR LESS

A 40-DAY DEVOTIONAL

MAX LUCADO

THOMAS NELSON
Since 1798

NASHVILLE   DALLAS   MEXICO CITY   RIO DE JANEIRO

© 2009 by Thomas Nelson, Inc.

All rights reserved. No portion of this book may be reproduced, stored in a retrieval system, or transmitted in any form or by any means—electronic, mechanical, photocopy, recording, scanning, or other—except for brief quotations in critical reviews or articles, without the prior written permission of the publisher.

Published in Nashville, Tennessee, by Thomas Nelson. Thomas Nelson is a registered trademark of Thomas Nelson, Inc.

Thomas Nelson, Inc. titles may be purchased in bulk for educational, business, fundraising, or sales promotional use. For information, please email NelsonMinistryServices@ThomasNelson.com.

All Scripture references, unless otherwise noted, are from THE NEW KING JAMES VERSION® (NKJV) © 1982 Thomas Nelson, Inc. Used by permission. All rights reserved. The New International Version of the Bible (NIV). Copyright © 1984 International Bible Society. Used by permission of Zondervan Bible Publishers. New American Standard Bible (NASB). Copyright © The Lockman Foundation, 1995. Used by permission. Holy Bible, New Living Translation (NLT) © 199, 2004. Used by permission of Tyndale House Publishers, Inc., Wheaton, Illinois 60189. The Contemporary English Version (CEV) © 1995 American Bible Society. Used by permission.

Cover and interior design by Kristy Morell, Smyrna, Tennessee

ISBN-13: 9788031452791

Printed in the United States of America

DAY 1

*But Jesus spoke to them at once. "Don't be
afraid," he said. "Take courage. I am here!"
Then Peter called to him, "Lord, if it's
really you, tell me to come to you, walking
on the water." "Yes, come," Jesus said.
So Peter went over the side of the boat and
walked on the water toward Jesus.*

MATTHEW 14:27–29 NLT

When fear shapes our lives, safety becomes our
god. When safety becomes our god, we worship the risk-free life. Can the safety lover do anything great? Can the risk-averse accomplish noble
deeds? For God? For others? No. The fear-filled cannot love deeply. Love is risky. They cannot give to
the poor. Benevolence has no guarantee of return.
The fear-filled cannot dream wildly. What if their
dreams sputter and fall from the sky? The worship
of safety emasculates greatness. No wonder Jesus
wages such a war against fear.

Imagine Your Life Without Fear

DAY 2

*These things I have spoken to you, that in Me
you may have peace. In the world you will
have tribulation; but be of good cheer,
I have overcome the world.*

JOHN 16:33 NKJV

The Gospels list some 125 Christ-issued impera-
tives. Of these, 21 urge us to "not be afraid" or
"not fear" or "have courage" or "take heart" or "be
of good cheer." The second most common com-
mand, to love God and neighbor, appears on only
eight occasions. If quantity is any indicator, Jesus
takes our fears seriously. The one statement he
made more than other was this: don't be afraid.

Fearless

4

Day 3

When I am afraid, I put my trust in you.

Psalm 56:3, nlt

How did Jesus endure the terror of the crucifixion? He went first to the Father with his fears.

Do the same with yours. Don't avoid life's Gardens of Gethsemane. Enter them. Just don't enter them alone. And while there, be honest. Pounding the ground is permitted. Tears are allowed. . . . And be specific. . . . He knows what you need.

Everyday Blessings

Day 4

You shall receive power when the Holy Spirit has come upon you.

ACTS 1:8, NKJV

Remember the followers' fear at the crucifixion? They ran. Scared as cats in a dog pound....

But fast-forward forty days.... Peter is preaching in the very precinct where Christ was arrested. Followers of Christ defy the enemies of Christ.... As bold after the Resurrection as they were cowardly before it.

Explanation? A resurrected Christ and his Holy Spirit. The courage of these men and women was forged in the fire of the empty tomb.

Eveyrday Blesssings

Day 5

The Spirit himself bears witness with
our Spirit that we are children of God.

ROMANS 8:16 NASB

When we come to Christ, God not only forgives us, he also adopts us. Through a dramatic series of events, we go from condemned orphans with no hope to adopted children with no fear. Here is how it happens. You come before the judgment seat of God full of rebellion and mistakes. Because of his justice he cannot dismiss your sin, but because of his love he cannot dismiss you. So, in an act which stunned the heavens, he punished himself on the cross for your sins. God's justice and love are equally honored. And you, God's creation, are forgiven. But the story doesn't end with God's forgiveness. . . .

It would be enough if God just cleansed your name, but he does more. He gives you *his* name.

The Great House of God

Day 6

So let us come boldly to the throne of our gracious God. There we will receive his mercy, and we will find grace to help us when we need it most.

Jesus tells us … ,"When you pray, pray like this. 'Our Father who is in heaven, hallowed be thy name. Thy kingdom come.'"

When you say, "Thy kingdom come," you are inviting the Messiah himself to walk into your world. "Come, my King! Take your throne in our land. Be present in my heart. Be present in my office. Come into my marriage. Be Lord of my family, my fears, and my doubts." This is no feeble request; it's a bold appeal for God to occupy every corner of your life.

[And] who are you to ask such a thing? Who are you to ask God to take control of your world? You are his child, for heaven's sake! And so you ask boldly.

The Great House of God

DAY 7

If God is for us, who can be against us?

ROMANS 8:31 NIV

The question is not simply, "Who can be against us?" You could answer that one. Who is against you? Disease, inflation, corruption, exhaustion. Calamities confront, and fears imprison. Were Paul's question, "Who can be against us?" we could list our foes much easier than we could fight them. But that is not the question. The question is, If GOD IS FOR US, *who can be against us?*

God is for you. Your parents may have forgotten you, your teachers may have neglected you, your siblings may be ashamed of you; but within reach of your prayers is the maker of the oceans. God!

In the Grip of Grace

DAY 8

I am the LORD your God. I am holding your hand,
so don't be afraid. I am here to help you.

ISAIAH 41:13 CEV

Could you use some courage? Are you backing down more than you are standing up? Jesus scattered the butterflies out of the stomachs of his nervous disciples. . . .

We need to remember that the disciples were common men given a compelling task. Before they were the stained-glassed saints in the windows of cathedrals, they were somebody's next-door-neighbors trying to make a living and raise a family. They weren't cut from theological cloth or raised on supernatural milk. But they were an ounce more devoted than they were afraid and, as a result, did some extraordinary things.

Earthly fears are no fears at all. Answer the big question of eternity, and the little questions of life fall into perspective.

The Applause of Heaven

DAY 9

About midnight Paul and Silas
were praying and singing songs to God
as the other prisoners listened.

ACTS 16:25 NCV

Great acts of faith are seldom born out of calm
calculation. It wasn't logic that caused Moses
to raise his staff on the bank of the Red Sea. It was-
n't medical research that convinced Naaman to dip
seven times in the river. It wasn't common sense
that caused Paul to abandon the Law and embrace
grace.

And it wasn't a confident committee that prayed
in a small room in Jerusalem for Peter's release from
prison. It was a fearful, desperate, band of backed-
into-a-corner believers. It was a church with no
options. A congregation of have-nots pleading for
help. And never were they stronger. At the begin-
ning of every act of faith, there is often a seed of fear.

In the Eye of the Storm

Day 10

Lord, show us the Father.
That is all we need.

John 14:8 cev

Biographies of bold disciples begin with chapters of honest terror. Fear of death. Fear of failure. Fear of loneliness. Fear of a wasted life. Fear of failing to know God.

Faith begins when you see God on the mountain and you are in the valley and you know that you're too weak to make the climb. You see what you need . . . you see what you have . . . and what you have isn't enough to accomplish anything. . . .

Moses had a sea in front and an enemy behind. The Israelites could swim or they could fight. But neither option was enough. . . .

Paul had mastered the Law. He had mastered the system. But one glimpse of God convinced him that sacrifice and symbols were not enough. . . . Faith that begins with fear will end up nearer the Father.

In the Eye of the Storm

DAY 11

The LORD is my light and
my salvation; whom shall I fear?

PSALM 27:1 NIV

Jesus says the options are clear. On one side there is the voice of safety. You can build a fire in the hearth, stay inside, and stay warm and dry for what you don't try, right? You can't fall if you don't take a stand, right? You can't lose your balance if you never climb, right? So don't try it. Take the safe route.

Or you can hear the voice of adventure—God's adventure. Instead of building a fire in your hearth, build a fire in your heart. Follow God's impulses. Adopt the child. Move overseas. Teach the class. Change careers. Run for office. Make a difference. Sure it isn't safe, but what is?

He Still Moves Stones

DAY 12

Where God's love is, there is no fear,
because God's perfect love drives out fear.

1 JOHN 4:18 NCV

A lot of us live with a hidden fear that God is angry at us. Somewhere, sometime, some Sunday school class or some television show convinced us that God has a whip behind his back, a paddle in his back pocket, and he's going to nail us when we've gone too far.

No concept could be more wrong! Our Savior's Father is very fond of us and only wants to share his love with us. We have a Father who is filled with compassion, a feeling Father who hurts when his children hurt. We serve a God who says that even when we're under pressure and feel like nothing is going to go right, he is waiting for us, to embrace us whether we succeed or fail.

He doesn't come quarreling and wrangling and forcing his way into anyone's heart. He comes into our hearts like a gentle lamb, not a roaring lion.

Walking with the Savior

Day 13

Then you will experience God's peace,
which exceeds anything we can understand.
His peace will guard your hearts and
minds as you live in Christ Jesus.

Philippians 4:7 NLT

The disciples fretted over the need to feed the thousands, but not Jesus. He thanked God for the problem. The disciples shouted for fear in the storm, but not Jesus. He slept through it. Peter drew his sword to fight the soldiers, but not Jesus. He lifted his hand to heal. His heart was at peace. When his disciples abandoned him, did he pout and go home? When Peter denied him, did Jesus lose his temper? When the soldiers spit in his face, did he breathe fire in theirs? Far from it. He was at peace. He forgave them. He refused to be guided by vengeance. What are you guided by?

Just Like Jesus

DAY 14

*But Jesus spoke to them at once. "Don't be
afraid," he said. "Take courage. I am here*

MATTHEW 14:27 NLT

A ghost," someone screamed. Fear of the sea was
eclipsed by a new terror. Thoughts raced as the
specter drew near. Was it a figment of our imagination? Was it a vision? Who? How? What was this
mystical light that appeared so … ?

A flash of lightning illuminated the sky. For a second I could see its face … his face. A second was all
I needed. It was the Master! He spoke:

"Take courage! It is I. Don't be afraid."

Nothing had changed. The storm still raged. The
wind still shrieked. The boat still pitched. The thunder still boomed. The rain still slapped. But in the
midst of the tumult, I could hear his voice. The
night was ferocious, yet he spoke as though the sea
were placid and the sky silent.

And, somehow, courage came. Let your heart
and mind be filled with courage because Jesus is
saying, "Take courage! It is I. Don't be afraid."

In the Eye of the Storm

DAY 15

On the evening of that first day of the week,
when the disciples were together,
with the doors locked for fear of the Jews . . .

JOHN 20:19 NIV

The church of Jesus Christ began with a group of frightened men in a second-floor room in Jerusalem. Though trained and taught, they didn't know what to say. Though they'd marched with him for three years, they now sat … afraid. They were timid soldiers, reluctant warriors, speechless messengers. Their most courageous act was to get up and lock the door.

Some looked out the window, some looked at the wall, some looked at the floor, but all looked inside themselves. And well they should, for it was an hour of self-examination. All their efforts seemed so futile. Nagging their memories were the promises they'd made but not kept. When the Roman soldiers took Jesus, Jesus' followers took off. With the very wine of the covenant on their breath and the bread of his sacrifice in their bellies, they fled.

Six Hours One Friday

Day 16

And he said, "O man greatly beloved, fear not!
Peace be to you; be strong, yes, be strong!"
So when he spoke to me I was strengthened,
and said, "Let my lord speak,
for you have strengthened me."

Daniel 10:19 NKJV

All those boasts of bravado? All those declarations of devotion? They lay broken and shattered at the gate of Gethsemane's garden. We don't know where the disciples went when they fled the garden, but we do know what they took: a memory. They took a heart-stopping memory of a man who called himself no less than God in the flesh. And they couldn't get him out of their minds.

No, they couldn't forget him. As a result, they came back. And, as a result, the church of our Lord began with a group of frightened men in an upper room.

Six Hours One Friday

18

DAY 17

*The Spirit will teach you everything and will
remind you of what I said while I was with you.
I give you peace, the kind of peace that only
I can give. It isn't like the peace that this
world can give. So don't be worried or afraid.*

JOHN 14:26–27 CEV

Upper-room futility. Confused ambassadors behind locked doors. What will it take to unlock them? What will it take to ignite the fire? What will it take to restore the first-century passion?

What will have to happen before the padlocks of futility tumble from our doors and are trampled under the feet of departing disciples? More training? That's part of it. A greater world vision? Undoubtedly. More money? That's imperative. A greater dependence on the Holy Spirit? Absolutely.

There is one element so vital that its absence ensures our failure. What is needed to get us out is exactly what got the apostles out. . . . they saw Jesus.

Six Hours One Friday

DAY 18

I am telling you this before I leave, so that when it does happen, you will have faith in me. I cannot speak with you much longer, because the ruler of this world is coming. But he has no power over me.

JOHN 14:29–30 CEV

Picture the scene. Peter, John, James. They came back . . . Daring to dream that the master had left them some word, some plan, some direction, they came back.

But little did they know their wildest dream wasn't wild enough. Just as someone mumbles, "It's no use," they hear a noise. They hear a voice.

"Peace be with you." Someone looked at the door.

It was still locked. The one betrayed sought his betrayers. What did he say to them? Not "What a bunch of flops!" Not "I told you so." No "Where-were-you-when-I-needed-you?" speeches. But simply one phrase, "Peace be with you." The very thing they didn't have was the very thing he offered: peace.

Six Hours One Friday

DAY 19

I will forgive their wickedness
and will remember their sins no more.

HEBREWS 8:12 NIV

"Therefore, there is now no condemnation for those who are in Christ Jesus" (Romans 8:1 NIV).

"[God] justifies those who have faith in Jesus" (Romans 3:26 NIV).

For those in Christ, these promises are not only a source of joy. They are also the foundations of true courage. You are guaranteed that your sins will be filtered through, hidden in, and screened out by the sacrifice of Jesus. When God looks at you, he doesn't see you; he sees the One who surrounds you. That means that failure is not a concern for you. Your victory is secure. How could you not be courageous?

The Applause of Heaven

DAY 20

*I have learned the secret
of being happy at any time in
everything that happens.*

PHILIPPIANS 4:12 CEV

Peer into the prison and see [Paul] for yourself: bent and frail, shackled to the arm of a Roman guard. Behold the apostle of God....

Dead broke. No family. No property. Nearsighted and worn out. . . . Doesn't look like a hero.

Doesn't sound like one either. He introduced himself as the worst sinner in history. He was a Christian-killer before he was a Christian leader. At times his heart was so heavy, Paul's pen drug itself across the page. "What a miserable man I am! Who will save me from this body that brings me death?" (Rom. 7:24).

Only heaven knows how long he stared at the question before he found the courage to defy logic and write, "I thank God for saving me through Jesus Christ our Lord!" (Rom. 7:25).

When God Whispers Your Name

DAY 21

I am the Lord your God, who holds
your right hand, and I tell you,
"Don't be afraid. I will help you."

ISAIAH 41:13 CEV

Could you use some courage? Are you backing down more than you are standing up? Jesus scattered the butterflies out of the stomachs of his nervous disciples. . . .

We need to remember that the disciples were common men given a compelling task. Before they were the stained-glassed saints in the windows of cathedrals, they were somebody's next-door-neighbors trying to make a living and raise a family. They weren't cut from theological cloth or raised on supernatural milk. But they were an ounce more devoted than they were afraid and, as a result, did some extraordinary things.

Earthly fears are no fears at all. Answer the big question of eternity, and the little questions of life fall into perspective.

The Applause of Heaven

DAY 22

Take courage, it is I; do not be afraid.

MATTHEW 14:27, NASB

Waves slapping his waist and rain stinging his face. Jesus speaks to [the disciples] at once. "Courage! I am! Don't be afraid!"

Speaking from a burning bush to a knee-knocking Moses, God announced, "I AM WHO I AM" (Exod. 3:14, NASB).

God gets into things! Red Seas…. Judean wildernesses, weddings, funerals, and Galilean tempests. Look and you'll find what everyone from Moses to Martha discovered. God in the middle of our storms.

Everyday Blessings

Day 23

*It is not the healthy people
who need a doctor, but the sick....
I did not come to invite good people
but to invite sinners.*

Matthew 9:12–13 ncv

God didn't look at our frazzled lives and say, "I'll die for you when you deserve it."

No, despite our sin, in the face of our rebellion, he chose to adopt us. And for God, there's no going back. His grace is a come-as-you-are promise from a one-of-a-kind King. You've been found, called, and adopted; so trust your Father and claim this verse as your own: "God showed his love for us in this way: Christ died for us while we were still sinners" (Rom. 5:8). And you never again have to wonder who your father is—you've been adopted by God and are therefore an "heir of God through Christ" (Gal. 4:7).

In the Grip of Grace

DAY 24

*Faith means being sure of the things
we hope for and knowing that something is real
even if we do not see it.*

HEBREWS 11:1 NCV

Faith is trusting what the eye can't see.

Eyes see the prowling lion. Faith sees Daniel's
angel.

Eyes see storms. Faith sees Noah's rainbow.

Eyes see giants. Faith sees Canaan.

Your eyes see your faults. Your faith sees your
Savior.

Your eyes see your guilt. Your faith sees his blood.

Your eyes look in the mirror and see a sinner, a
failure, a promise-breaker. But by faith you
look in the mirror and see a robed prodigal
bearing the ring of grace on your finger and
the kiss of your Father on your face.

When God Whispers Your Name

DAY 25

The person who trusts
the LORD will be blessed.

JEREMIAH 17:7 NCV

J ust prior to his crucifixion, [Jesus] told his disciples that he would be leaving them. "Where I am going you cannot follow now, but you will follow later" (John 13:36).

Such a statement was bound to stir some questions. Peter spoke for the others and asked, "Lord, why can't I follow you now?" (v. 37).

See if Jesus' reply doesn't reflect the tenderness of a parent to a child: "Don't let your hearts be troubled. Trust in God, and trust in me. There are many rooms in my Father's house; I would not tell you this it if were not true. I am going there to prepare a place for you.... I will come back and take you to be with me so that you may be where I am going" (John 14:1–3).

Reduce the paragraph to a sentence and it might read: "You do the trusting and I'll do the taking."

When Christ Comes

Day 26

*I will praise You, for I am fearfully
and wonderfully made;
Marvelous are Your works,
And that my soul knows very well.*

Psalm 139:14 NKJV

Fear of insignificance creates the result it dreads,
arrives at the destination it tries to avoid, facilitates the scenario it disdains. If you pass your days
mumbling, "I'll never make a difference; I'm not
worth anything," guess what? You will be sentencing yourself to a life of gloom without parole.

Even more, you are disagreeing with God. Questioning His judgement. Second-guessing His taste.
According to Him you were "skillfully wrought."
You were "fearfully and wonderfully made." He can't
stop think about you! If you could count His
thoughts of you, "they would be more in number
than the sand" (Psalm 139:18).

Fearless

28

Day 27

For we are God's masterpiece. He has created
us anew in Christ Jesus,
so we can do the good things
he planned for us long ago

EPHESIANS 2:10 NLT

Why does he love you so much? The same reason the artist loves his paintings or the boat builder loves his vessels. You are His idea. And God has only good ideas. "For we are God's masterpiece. He has created us anew in Christ Jesus, so we can do the good things He planned for us long ago."

Fearless

DAY 28

Don't you even fear God when you are dying? We deserve to die for our evil deeds, but this man hasn't done one thing wrong.

LUKE 23:40–41 NLT

Lodged in the thief's statement are two facts that anyone needs to recognize in order to come to Jesus. Do you see them?

"We are getting what we deserve. This man has done nothing wrong. We are guilty and he is innocent. We are filthy and he is pure. We are wrong and he is right. He is not on that cross for his sins. He is there for ours. . . ."

At this point Jesus performs the greatest miracle of the cross. Greater than the earthquake. Greater than the tearing of the temple curtain. Greater than the darkness, Greater than the resurrected saints appearing on the streets. He performs the miracle of forgiveness. A sin-soaked criminal is received by a blood-stained Savior.

Six Hours One Friday

Day 29

I will forgive their wickedness
and will remember their sins no more.

Hebrews 8:12 NIV

"Therefore, there is now no condemnation for those who are in Christ Jesus" (Romans 8:1 NIV).

"[God] justifies those who have faith in Jesus" (Romans 3:26 NIV).

For those in Christ, these promises are not only a source of joy. They are also the foundations of true courage. You are guaranteed that your sins will be filtered through, hidden in, and screened out by the sacrifice of Jesus. When God looks at you, he doesn't see you; he sees the One who surrounds you. That means that failure is not a concern for you. Your victory is secure. How could you not be courageous?

Grace for the Moment

DAY 30

Christ rose first; then when
Christ comes back, all his people
will become alive again.

1 CORINTHIANS 15:23 TLB

God has made [a] promise to us. "I will come back ... ," he assures us. Yes, the rocks will tumble. Yes, the ground will shake. But the child of God needn't fear—for the Father has promised to take us to be with him.

But dare we believe the promise? Dare we trust his loyalty? Isn't there a cautious part of us that wonders how reliable these words may be? ...

How can we know he will do what he said? How can we believe he will move the rocks and set us free?

Because he's already done it once.

When Christ Comes

DAY 31

Trust the LORD with all your heart,
and don't depend on your own understanding.

PROVERBS 3:5 NCV

The problem with this world is that it doesn't fit. Oh, it will do for now, but it isn't tailor-made. We were made to live with God, but on earth we live by faith.

We must trust God. We must trust not only that he does what is best but that he knows what is ahead. Ponder the words of Isaiah 57:1–2: "The good men perish; the godly die before their time and no one seems to care or wonder why. No one seems to realize that God is taking them away from the evil days ahead. For the godly who die shall rest in peace" (TLB).

My, what a thought. God is taking them away from the evil days ahead. Could death be God's grace? Could the funeral wreath be God's safety ring? As horrible as the grave may be, could it be God's protection from the future?

Trust in God, Jesus urges, and trust in me.

A Gentle Thunder

Day 32

He is my defender; I will not be defeated.

Here is a big question. What is God doing when you are in a bind? When the lifeboat springs a leak? When the rip cord snaps? When the last penny is gone before the last bill is paid? …

I know what we are doing. Nibbling on nails like corn on the cob. Pacing floors. Taking pills.…

But what does God do? …

He fights for us. He steps into the ring and points us to our corner and takes over. "Remain calm; the Lord will fight for you" (Exod. 14:14).

His job is to fight. Our job is to trust.

Just trust. Not direct. Or question.… Our job is to pray and wait.

When God Whispers Your Name

DAY 33

Surely I spoke of things I did not understand;
I talked of things too wonderful for me to know.

JOB 42:3 NCV

It's easy to thank God when he does what we want. But God doesn't always do what we want. Ask Job.

His empire collapsed, his children were killed, and what was a healthy body became a rage of boils. From whence came this torrent? From whence will come any help?

Job goes straight to God and pleads his case. His head hurts. His body hurts. His heart hurts.

And God answers. Not with answers but with questions. An ocean of questions....

After several dozen questions ... Job has gotten the point. What is it?

The point is this: God owes no one anything. No reasons. No explanations. Nothing. If he gave them, we couldn't understand them.

God is God. He knows what he is doing. When you can't trace his hand, trust his heart.

The Inspirational Study Bible

DAY 34

*I leave you peace; my peace
I give you. I do not give it to you
as the world does. So don't let your
hearts be troubled or afraid.*

JOHN 14:27 NCV

If only you knew that I came to help and not con-
demn. If only you knew that tomorrow will be
better than today. If only you knew the gift I have
brought: eternal life. If only you knew I want you
safely home.

If only you knew.

What wistful words to come from the lips of
God. How kind that he would let us hear them.
How crucial that we pause to hear them. If only we
knew to trust. Trust that God is in our corner. Trust
that God wants what is best....

If only we could learn to trust him.

A Gentle Thunder

DAY 35

*. . . The appearance of his face was transformed,
and his clothes became dazzling white. Suddenly,
two men, Moses and Elijah, appeared and began
talking with Jesus. They were glorious to see.
And they were speaking about his exodus from this
world, which was about to be fulfilled in Jerusalem.*

LUKE 9:29–31

When Christ is great, our fears are not. As awe
of Jesus expands, fears of life diminish. A big
God translates into big courage. A small view of
God generates no courage.

This must be why Jesus took the disciples up the
mountain. He saw the box in which they had con-
fined him. He saw the future that awaited them: the
fireside denial of Peter, prisons of Jerusalem and
Rome, demand of the church, and the persecutions
of Nero. A box-sized version of God simply would
not work. So Jesus blew the sides out the disciple's
preconceptions. Let Him blow the sides of our yours!

Fearless

DAY 36

"I am going away."

JOHN 14:28 NKJV

Imagine their shock when they heard Jesus say those words. He spoke them on the night of the Passover celebration, Thursday evening in the Upper Room. Christ and his friends had just enjoyed a calm dinner in the midst of a chaotic week. They had freason for optimism: Jesus' popularity was soaring. Opportunities were increasing. In three short years the crowds had lifted Christ to their shoulders . . . he was the hope of the common man. And now this? Jesus said, "I am going away." The announcement stunned them. When Jesus explained, "you know the way to where I am going," Thomas replied, "No, we don't know Lord. We have no idea where you are going, so how can we know the way?

Fearless

DAY 37

But when the Father sends the Advocate as my representative—that is, the Holy Spirit—he will teach you everything and will remind you of everything I have told you.

John 14:26 nlt

On the eve of his death, Jesus gave his followers this promise found in John 14:26 & 27. Counselor means "friend" (MSG), "helper" (NKJV), "intercessor, advocate, strengthener, standby" (AMP). All descriptors attempt to portray the beautiful meaning of parakletos, a compound of two Greek words. Para means "alongside of". Kletos means "to be called out, designated, assigned or appointed." The Holy spirit is designated to come alongside you. He is the presence of Jesus with and in the followers of Jesus.

Fearless

Day 38

I am leaving you with a gift—peace
of mind and heart. And the peace
I give is a gift the world cannot give.
So don't be troubled or afraid

John 14:27 nlt

It's Thursday night before the crucifixion. By Friday's sunrise they will abandon Jesus. The breakfast hour will find them hiding in corners and crevices. At 9 a.m. Roman soldiers will nail Christ to a cross. By the time tomorrow he will be dead and buried. Their world is about to be flipped on its head. And Jesus wants them to know: they'll never face the future without his help. Nor will you. You have a travel companion.

Fearless

Day 39

Remember what I told you:
I am going away, but I
will come back to you again.
If you really loved me, you
would be happy that I am
going to the Father, who is
greater than I am. I have told you these
things before they happen so that when
they do happen, you will believe.

John 14:28–29 NLT

When you place your faith in Christ, Christ places his Spirit before, behind, and within you. Everything Jesus did for His followers, his Spirit does for you. Jesus taught; the Spirit teaches, Jesus healed; the Spirit heals. Jesus comforted; his Spirit comforts. As Jesus sends you into new seasons, he sends his Counselor to go with you.

Fearless

DAY 40

You shall receive power when
the Holy Spirit has come upon you.

ACTS 1:8, NKJV

Remember the followers' fear at the crucifixion? They ran. Scared as cats in a dog pound. . . .

But fast-forward forty days. . . . Peter is preaching in the very precinct where Christ was arrested. Followers of Christ defy the enemies of Christ. . . . As bold after the Resurrection as they were cowardly before it.

Explanation? A resurrected Christ and his Holy Spirit. The courage of these men and women was forged in the fire of the empty tomb.

Grace for the Moment

EXCERPT FROM
OUTLIVE YOUR LIFE

*Let the empty tomb forge the
fire in your own heart and life.*

You want your life to matter. You want to live in such a way that the world will be glad you did.

But how can you? How can I? Can God use us?

I have one hundred-and-twenty answers to that question. One hundred and twenty residents of ancient Israel. They were charter members of the Jerusalem church (see Acts 1:15). Fishermen, some. Revenue reps, others. A former streetwalker and a converted terrorist or two. They had no clout with Caesar, no friends at the temple headquarters. Truth be told, they had nothing more than this: a fire in the belly to change the world.

Thanks to Luke, we know how they fared. He recorded their stories in the book of Acts. Let's listen to it. That's right—listen to the book of Acts. It cracks with the sounds of God's ever-expanding work. Press your ear against the pages and hear God press into the corners and crevices of the world.

Hear sermons echo off the temple walls. Baptistery

waters splashing, just-saved souls laughing. Hear the spoon scrape the bowl as yet another hungry mouth is fed.

Listen to the doors opening and walls collapsing. Doors to Antioch, Ethiopia, Corinth, and Rome. Doors into palaces, prisons, and Roman palisades.

And walls. The ancient prejudice between Jew and Samaritan—down! The thick and spiked division between Jew and Gentile—crash! The partitions that quarantined male from female, landowner from pauper, master from slave, black African from Mediterranean Jew—God demolishes them all.

Acts announces, "God is afoot!"

Is he still? we wonder. *Would God do with us what he did with his first followers?*

Heaven knows we hope so. These are devastating times: 3 billion people are desperately poor, 1 billion are hungry, millions are trafficked in slavery, pandemic diseases are gouging entire nations. In the five minutes it took you to read these pages, ninety children died of preventable diseases. More than half of all Africans do not have access to modern health facilities. As a result, ten million people die each year from diarrhea, acute respiratory illness, malaria, and measles. All for the lack of vaccines.[1] Each year more than 2 million children are exploited in the global commercial sex trade.[2]

Yet, in the midst of the wreckage, here we stand, the

modern-day version of the Jerusalem church. You, me, and our one-of-a-kind lifetimes and once-in-history opportunity.

Ours is the wealthiest generation of Christians ever. We are bright, educated, and experienced. We can travel around the world in twenty-four hours or send a message in a millisecond. We have the most sophisticated research and medicines at the tips of our fingers. We have ample resources. A mere 2 percent of the world's grain harvest would be enough, if shared, to erase the problem of hunger and malnutrition around the world. There is enough food on the planet to offer every person twenty-five hundred calories of sustenance a day. We have enough food to feed the hungry.

And we have enough bedrooms to house the orphans. Here's the math. There are 145 million orphans world-wide. More than 239 million people in the US call themselves Christians. From a purely statistical standpoint, American Christians by themselves have the wherewith-all to house every orphan in the world.

Of course, many people are not in a position to do so. They are elderly, infirm, unemployed, or simply feel no call to adopt. Yet, what if a small percentage of them did? A percentage of, hmmm, let's say 6 percent. If so, we could provide loving homes for the 14.1 million children in sub-Saharan Africa who have been orphaned by the AIDS epidemic.[3] Among the noble causes of the church, how does that one sound? "American Christians Stand Up for AIDS Orphans." Wouldn't that headline be a welcome one?

I don't mean to oversimplify these terribly complicated questions. We can't just snap our fingers and expect the grain to flow across borders or governments to permit foreign adoptions. Policies stalemate the best of efforts. International relations are strained. Corrupt officials snag the systems. I get that.

But this much is clear: the storehouse is stocked. The problem is not in the supply; the problem is in the distribution. God has given this generation, our generation, everything we need to alter the course of human suffering.

Join us and
OUTLIVE YOUR LIFE
Available Fall 2010
1-800-933-9673

26,000 per day
[1] *The Poor Will be Glad* Peter Greer and Phil Smith p. 26 Zondervan 2009
[2] See International Justice Mission home page
        sider, p. 10
        Sider, p. 35
        source: *UNICEF*, 2006
        www.adherents.com/re_USA.html
[3] www.worldvision.org

BIBLIOGRAPHY

The Applause of Heaven, (Nashville: Thomas Nelson, Inc. 2008)

Everyday Blessings, (Nashville: Thomas Nelson, Inc. 2004)

Fearless, (Nashville: Thomas Nelson, Inc. 2009)

A Gentle Thunder, (Nashville: Thomas Nelson, Inc. 2009)

Grace for the Moment, (Nashville: Thomas Nelson, Inc. 2008)

The Great House of God, (Nashville: Thomas Nelson, Inc. 2001)

He Still Moves Stones, (Nashville: Thomas Nelson, Inc. 2009)

Imagine Your Life Without Fear, (Nashville: Thomas Nelson, Inc. 2008)

In the Eye of the Storm, (Nashville: Thomas Nelson, Inc. 2009)

In the Grip of Grace, (Nashville: Thomas Nelson, Inc. 2005)

The Inspirational Study Bible, (Nashville: Thomas Nelson, Inc. 1997)

Just Like Jesus, (Nashville: Thomas Nelson, Inc. 2008)

Six Hours One Friday, (Nashville: Thomas Nelson, Inc. 2009)

Walking with the Savior, (Nashville: Thomas Nelson, Inc. 2009)

When Christ Comes, (Nashville: Thomas Nelson, Inc. 2001)

When God Whispers Your Name, (Nashville: Thomas Nelson, Inc. 1999)

To order additional copies
call 1-800-933-9673
or visit
www.nelsonministryservices.com